WHEN
JOY
CAME

WHEN JOY CAME

THE STORY OF THE FIRST CHRISTMAS

by Pauline Palmer Meek

illustrated by Shannon Stirnweis

Fifth Printing, 1977

0-307-10887-2

gb

GOLDEN PRESS
Western Publishing Company, Inc.
Racine, Wisconsin

Joseph and Mary were traveling to Bethlehem. They had to walk over hills, across streams, and down a long, winding road.

They had brought food and bedding for camping along the way. A sturdy donkey carried their things. They went past busy towns and growing gardens and rocky ridges.

Joseph was taking a vacation from his carpenter shop, because there was a new law which said he must register in Bethlehem to pay his taxes.

Mary might have wished to stay at home in Nazareth. She was expecting a baby. But Joseph had to go to Bethlehem. Of course Mary wanted to go with him.

How glad they were when they climbed the last steep hill and saw the town!

There were many other people who had already come
to Bethlehem to register.

Packtrains stopped there, too, for rest and water. The
courtyard was full of braying donkeys and snorting camels
and their shouting drivers.

There was no room for Mary and Joseph at the inn.

The only place for them to stay was in a stable. It was not a very good place, but it was better than camping along the road.

Night came. The donkeys and camels and their drivers grew quiet. The whole town of Bethlehem was still.

On a hill outside the town, some men were guarding their sheep through the long, silent hours of darkness. Stars made the only light.

Then something extraordinary happened. A glorious brightness was shining all around them! An unknown being was with them! The shepherds were terrified.

"Don't be afraid," God's messenger said. "I have good news—news that will bring joy to all the people. The Lord is with you! Just now, in Bethlehem, a very special baby has been born. In Him, God has come to rescue His people. You will know Him by this sign—He is lying in a manger."

All at once there were many, many angels. How happy they were! What beautiful songs they sang! Then the brightness dimmed and faded away into the high sky. The angels had gone.

Once again, stars made the only light. The hillside was as quiet as if nothing had happened. The shepherds were so astonished, they hardly knew what to think. "Let us go!" one of them said. "Let us go right away into Bethlehem and find this baby the Lord has told us about!"

They went. They found Mary, and Joseph, and a tiny
baby. Just as the angel had said, the baby was lying in
a manger.

How happy the shepherds were to find Him! They knew
He was God's Chosen One.

How happy Joseph was! He knew, too, that this new-born boy would grow up to do great work.

How happy Mary was! Her baby was the most beautiful child that ever was born. When she held Him in her arms, she knew how truly wonderful Jesus was.
Joy! Joy! Joy!